001
Man and women of the mercantile class,
England, ca. 1600

002
James I of England and his queen,
Anne of Denmark, ca. 1610

003
King Henry IV of France and his queen,
Marie de Médicis, in formal court dress, ca. 1610

004
Jamestown settlers with a Native American, ca. 1607

005
King Henry IV of France, Marie de Médicis,
and their son, Louis (later Louis XIII), ca. 1610

006
English royal children, ca. 1610

007
Dutch aristocrats in court dress, ca. 1620

008
Pilgrim farm couple in North America, ca. 1610

009
English gentlemen, ca. 1614–16

010
English upper-middle-class family, ca. 1620

011
English and Dutch gentlemen at court, ca. 1620

012
French court clothes, ca. 1620

013
King Louis XIII of France and his favorite,
Charles de Luynes, ca. 1620

014
Dutch regent and his wife, ca. 1620–30

015
Puritans in North America, ca. 1620

016
Middle-class couple, France, ca. 1624

017
"Nouveau riche" middle class, France, ca. 1625

018
English country gentry, ca. 1630

019
A family of the Spanish court, ca. 1630

020
English theatrical costumes, ca. 1631

021
French court couple in promenade dance, ca. 1625

022
Dutch settlers in North America
skating on the Hudson River, ca. 1630

023
Dutch ladies of New Amsterdam, ca. 1630

024
Queen Henrietta Maria and
King Charles I of England, ca. 1633

025
French cavaliers, ca. 1630

026
French courtiers, ca. 1633

027
French and English soldiers, ca. 1636

028
French cavalier and lady, ca. 1640

029
French egg seller and water vendor, ca. 1640

030
Cavalier and Puritan, England, ca. 1645

031
Upper-middle-class Puritans, England, ca. 1645

032
Early Baroque fashions, France, ca. 1645

033
Royalist soldiers and a farm girl, England, ca. 1642–45

034
Parliamentary musketeer
and pikeman, England, ca. 1642–45

035
Contrasting styles—common
folk and aristocrat, France, ca. 1646

036
Oliver Cromwell with a Parliamentarian
and his wife, England, ca. 1646

037
English Puritan common folk, ca. 1650

038
French upper-class styles, ca. 1650

039
Townspeople in New Amsterdam, ca. 1650

040
Widow's costume, France, ca. 1660

041
American Puritans, ca. 1660

042
Dutch merchant-class couple, ca. 1660

043
Louis XIV of France and a court lady, ca. 1660

044
Charles II of England and
his sister, Mary Stuart, ca. 1660

045
A noble and his son in Restoration England, ca. 1663

046
Aristocratic mother and her
children in Restoration England, ca. 1663

047
Men's fashions, England, ca. 1666

048
French peasants, seventeenth century

049
Queen Maria Theresa of France, ca. 1670

050
A lady of the court and
King Louis XIV of France, ca. 1670

051
A palace guard and a musketeer,
France, ca. 1660–1700

052
King Louis XIV of France, ca. 1670

053
Wealthy Boston Pilgrim family, ca. 1674

054
Dutch-American couple in formal dress, ca. 1670

055
French-American farmers, ca. 1680–1700

056
French gentleman and lady, ca. 1680

057
Louis XIV of France and lady, ca. 1680

058
Lady of the French court, ca. 1680

059
Restoration gown and Puritan garb, England, ca. 1685

060
Wealthy Anglo-American
merchant couple, ca. 1685–1700

15

061
Madame de Maintenon, France, ca. 1690

062
French nobleman, ca. 1690

063
French nobleman and his son, ca. 1690

064
French noblewoman and her daughter, ca. 1690

065
French gentleman and lady "at home," ca. 1690–1710

066
Street scene, France, ca. 1700

067
Anglo-American townspeople—
laborers or artisans, ca. 1720–70

068
Changing French styles, ca. 1725

069
Anglo-American colonial
merchant couple, ca. 1725

070
Anglo-American colonial girls, ca. 1725–40

071
Strolling couple, France, ca. 1725

072
Fashionable French couple, ca. 1730

073
French gentleman and lady in latest styles, ca. 1730

074
Watteau gown with Chinese motif, France, ca. 1740

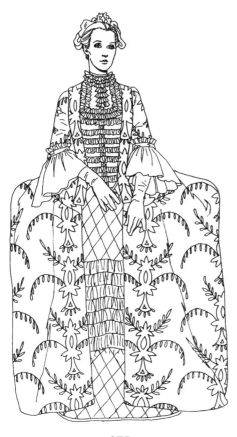

075
Anglo-American colonial lady, ca. 1746

076
Anglo-American colonial
lady in a formal gown, ca. 1740–50

077
Scottish immigrants in North America, ca. 1745

078
Robe á la Française, ca. 1750

079
Anglo-American colonial
shop girl or maid, ca. 1750–60

080
Anglo-American colonial couple, ca. 1750–75

081
Anglo-American colonists dancing, ca. 1750–65

082
Virginia settlers, ca. 1760–70

083
Colonial winter outerwear, ca. 1750–70

084
A colonial merchant and his family, ca. 1760–70

085
Stylish French couple, ca. 1760

086
Madame Pompadour, France, ca. 1760

087
Georgian gown, England, ca. 1760

088
Shepherdess style, France, ca. 1760

089
An English officer and a
colonial lady, North America, ca. 1760

090
North-American colonial
gentleman and lady, ca. 1770

091
Rococo gown, France, ca. 1775

092
Elaborate hairdo, court of
Marie Antoinette, France, ca. 1775

093
Court of Marie Antoinette
and Louis XVI, France, ca. 1776

094
Georgian England, "The Age of Reason," ca. 1780

095
French adaptation of English rural fashions, ca. 1780

096
English "sports," ca. 1781

097
British "Gainsborough" look, ca. 1785

098
French gentleman and lady, ca. 1789

099
Muscadine and lady, France, ca. 1792

100
Muscadine and lady, France, ca. 1793

101
Sansculotte and female
revolutionary, France, ca. 1793–94

102
Revolutionary street fighters, France, ca. 1793–94

103
Soldiers of the Directoire
and First Empire, France, ca. 1795

104
Soldiers, France, ca. 1795

105
Merchant and his daughters, France, ca. 1795

106
Merchant's wife and son, France, ca. 1795

107
Incroyables, France, ca. 1796

108
Merveilleuses, France, ca. 1796

109
Dance costumes, France, ca. 1796

110
Dance costumes, France, ca. 1796

111
Vendeuse and merchant, France, ca. 1796

112
Member of Directoire and lady, France, ca. 1799

113
Napoleon Bonaparte, France, ca. 1800

114
Gentleman and lady of the
First Empire, France, ca. 1800

115
French couple in walking costumes, ca. 1800

116
A well-dressed French couple, ca. 1800

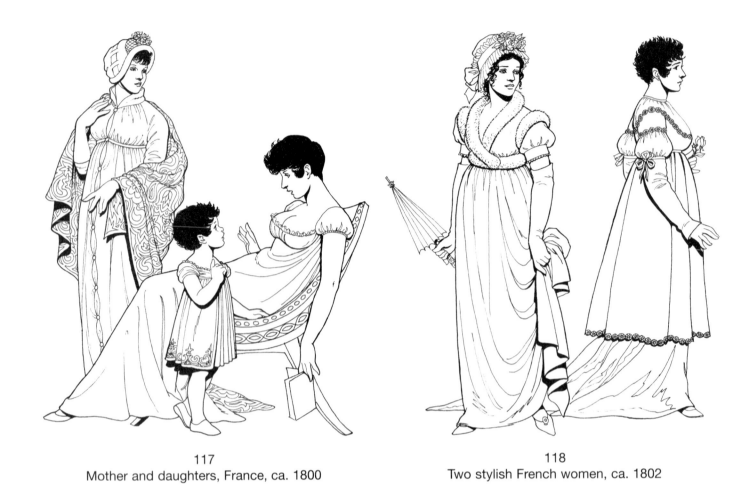

117
Mother and daughters, France, ca. 1800

118
Two stylish French women, ca. 1802

119
Evening wear, France, ca. 1803

120
French gentleman and lady, ca. 1804

121
Coronation of Empress Josephine, France, ca. 1804

122
Napoleon Bonaparte, France, ca. 1804

123
Emperor Napoleon Bonaparte
and Empress Josephine, France, ca. 1804

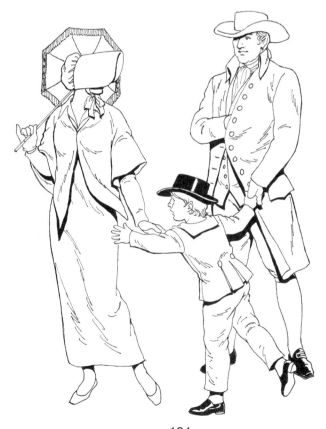

124
American Quakers, ca. 1804

125
French bride and groom, ca. 1805

126
George "Beau" Brummel, ca. 1805,
and Percy Bysshe Shelley, ca. 1820, England

127
French couple dressed for travel, ca. 1806

128
French lady and gentleman, ca. 1808

129
Young French couple in walking costume, ca. 1810

130
Fashionable women, France, ca. 1810

131
Three Empire evening gowns, France, ca. 1810

132
Couple out for a stroll, Franch, ca. 1810

133
Stylish French couple paying a call, ca. 1810

134
A fashionable French couple, ca. 1810

135
French couple in formal court dress, ca. 1813

136
Fur trim and ostrich plumes, France, ca. 1813

137
Two ladies wearing redingotes, France, ca. 1815

138
Family in formal day wear, France, ca. 1815

139
Day wear, Romantic period, ca. 1826

140
Evening wear, Romantic period, ca. 1829

141
Women's undergarments, Romantic period, ca. 1830

142
Men's undergarments, Romantic period, ca. 1830

143
Sleeve variations, Romantic period, ca. 1831

144
Boned corset, ca. 1837

145
Evening wear, ca. 1837

146
Day dress, ca. 1840

147
"Pre-Raphaelite" gowns, ca. 1840–70

148
Evening wear, ca. 1845

149
Day wear, ca. 1848

150
Evening wear, ca. 1849

151
Amelia Jenks Bloomer's "rational" costumes, ca. 1849

152
"Rational" evening wear, ca. 1850

153
Evening wear, ca. 1851

154
Lady's costume and child's dress, ca. 1852

155
Man's riding coat and lady's
fur-trimmed day cloak, ca. 1852

156
Woman's dress and man's
"Prince Albert" frock coat, ca. 1853

157
Crinoline dresses, ca. 1854

158
Crinoline walking dresses, ca. 1855

159
Bridal wear, ca. 1855

160
Promenade costumes, ca. 1856

161
Outdoor costumes, ca. 1857

162
Day wear, ca. 1857

163
"At-home" wear, ca. 1858

164
Lady's riding habit, ca. 1858

165
Woman and her children "at home," ca. 1859

166
Lady's promenade gown and
U.S. midshipman's uniform, ca. 1859

167
Carriage cloaks, ca. 1859

168
Day wear, ca. 1860

169
Lady's summer burnoose, ca. 1860

170
Patterned evening gown, ca. 1860

171
Woman and child, ca. 1861

172
Lady's opera cloak, ca. 1861

173
"Turkey back" jacket and walking dress ca. 1861–62

174
Woman and child, ca. 1862

175
Promenade costumes, ca. 1862

176
Walking costume, ca. 1863

177
Ice-skating costume, ca. 1863

178
Woman's day dress and U.S. Army uniforms, ca. 1864

179
Walking costume for the seaside, ca. 1865

180
Lady's Zouave-design robe and cape, ca. 1865

181
Lady's "Alexandra" dress and
U.S. Army captain's uniform, ca. 1865

182
Lady's military-styled dress and
Confederate Navy commander's uniform, ca. 1865

183
Winter promenade suit, ca. 1867

184
Ball gown, with crinoline hoop, ca. 1868

185
Evening dress, ca. 1873

186
Bridal gown, ca. 1876

187
Undergarments for evening gown with bustle, ca. 1878

188
Evening gown with bustle, ca. 1878

189
Bustled walking suit, ca. 1877

190
Bathing attire, ca. 1880

191
"Aesthetic Look," ca. 1882

192
Walking costumes, ca. 1884

193
American Victorian day wear, ca. 1885

194
Seaside attire, ca. 1886

195
Wedding attire, ca. 1890

196
Evening wear, ca. 1891

197
Cycling costumes, ca. 1894

198
Walking costumes, ca. 1895

199
Formal wear, ca. 1898

200
Dancing attire, ca. 1899

A SHORT HISTORY OF COSTUME

JACOBEAN AND EARLY BOURBON

The term "Jacobean" is often used to describe the era of the reign of James I, king of England (1603–1625), in which the preceding Elizabethan mode began to be phased out in favor of a return to classical Renaissance style. The heavy ornamentation and exaggerated silhouettes were gradually scaled back to a more understated look, which focused on the richness of fabrics. However, elements of Elizabethan clothing (which, in turn, borrowed heavily from Spanish fashion of the time) were still quite visible until the latter years of James's reign.

James's son, Charles I, took the throne in 1625 and married Henrietta Maria, the sister of France's king, Louis XIII, shortly thereafter. Charles was a patron of the arts and brought Flemish painters Anthony Van Dyck and Peter Paul Rubens to England as court painters. The influence of Flemish and French fashions can be seen in portraits of Charles by Van Dyck. His reign was tumultuous at best, thanks to neverending quarrels with Parliament and the Puritans, poor advice from his advisors, and a civil war. He was tried by a high court, convicted of treason, and beheaded in 1649.

Across the channel, Henry IV ruled as the first king of France in the Bourbon dynasty, which would last for two hundred years. Ascending the throne in 1589 and reigning for twenty-one years, he devoted his patronage to the vitalization of Paris, commissioning the creation of the Tuileries, the long gallery in the Louvre, and Place Dauphine. During most of his reign, court fashions were primarily influenced by Spanish styles as interpreted by his wife, Marie de Médicis, as well as those from Flanders and her native Italy. After Henry IV's assassination in 1610, his nine-year-old son, Louis XIII, became king, with his mother acting as regent until 1617. During his reign, which lasted until 1643, fashion in France was marked by the popularity of lace and simple lines.

CAVALIER, PURITAN, AND RESTORATION

During the latter years of James I's reign and that of his son, Charles I, the styles of England were heavily influenced by France because of the intermarriages of those countries' royal families. Under Louis XIII, France had established herself as the fashion arbiter of the world, and it was under his reign that the Cavalier style first came into vogue—a style that would become forever linked to England's Charles I. During the period 1625–1649 the padded stiffness of the Elizabethan era was replaced by a more casual, romantic look. Starch came out of the ruffs, bombast (padding) came out of doublets and hose, men's hair grew long, and women began discarding the farthingale. The unstarched ruff evolved into a wide collar or band; the doublet evolved into a jacket; and breeches, which were knee length with some fullness but no padding, replaced the trunk hose. Cloaks with wide collars and men's "Dutch"-styled broad-brimmed felt or beaver hats with long plumes and ribbons came into vogue. Women continued to wear constricting corsets, but farthingales and

hoops were out of fashion, with full skirts worn over several petticoats replacing them. Bosoms and shoulders were now seen, and for the first time in centuries fashionable women showed part of the arm under full sleeves that ended above the wrist. The simpler lines of the clothing for both men and women were reflected in a plainness of the rich fabrics. Fashionable folk wore both dark and light colors and a great deal of lace on their collars and cuffs.

A counterpoint to the extravagant court fashions was the sober garb worn by the Puritans. No one person can be credited with the birth of Protestantism, but the spread of ideas which led to it can be traced back to several outstanding personalities, among them Martin Luther (1483–1546), the German monk whose ideas about reforming the powerful Roman Catholic Church eventually led to the establishment of the Protestant Reformation. In England, Henry VIII's break with Rome (1534) further fanned the flames of the Protestant movement. His daughters, Mary (Catholic) and Elizabeth I (Protestant), would spend most of their reigns embroiled in power struggles between Catholic and Protestant factions. Elizabeth's successor, James I (son of the Catholic Mary, Queen of Scots) continued the religious balancing act. In France, the official religion was Roman Catholic, and many French Protestants fled to Holland and Switzerland for safety and asylum.

Holland had broken from Spanish Catholic rule in 1609 and was tolerant toward the religious refugees. Land poor, Holland had developed its mercantile trading and shipping industries and was quickly becoming the most prosperous country in the world. The predominantly Protestant Dutch merchant class's taste for simpler, less cumbersome, dress styles would have a great influence on Puritan garb. There were three distinct types of dress worn in Holland: Court dress that closely followed the latest French fashions; the "regent" class of wealthy merchant political leaders who preferred black clothes as a mark of their sober, pious authority; and, finally, the common folk who wore bits and pieces of used clothing previously worn by the upper classes. The Dutch regents greatly influenced the styles worn by the English Puritans.

Although Charles I is generally blamed for the events that led to the English Civil War, the seeds for war had been sown earlier by his father, who lost the trust of the merchant class via a series of foolish money-raising schemes, that destroyed England's clothing industry for over a generation. In 1625, Charles came to a bankrupted throne with a French Catholic wife, Henrietta Maria, and many Protestants feared that he would lead the country back to Catholicism. The Parliamentary party of the Civil War was composed not only of revolutionary peasants and religious fanatics, but also of people of all classes and walks of life. The most easily recognizable was the Puritan with his somber clothes and tall black hats.

After the execution of Charles I, England was declared a Commonwealth under the rule of Oliver Cromwell. The Commonwealth era was a period when unnecessary ornament on clothing was banished. Garments were simpler, more staid versions of court dress, though less generously cut and of more durable fabrics. The Puritan man wore a linen shirt and linen or cotton under-drawers. His breeches were cut fairly tightly and tied just below the knee with a simple self-fabric ribbon tie. Stockings were of worsted wool or cotton; shoes were square-toed and low heeled. The doublet had disappeared from fashion and the *justacorps* or coat became similar to the modern jacket, reaching to mid-thigh and buttoned all the way down the front, although some more style conscious men followed the court fashion of leaving the lower half unbuttoned. Severe linen collars were tied with strings and plain linen cuffs finished the sleeves. Hats had high crowns and flat brims. Most Puritan men had short hair, a style that earned them the soubriquet of "Roundhead." The overcoat made its first appearance and had a flat, squared collar and was cut full. Puritans preferred "sadde" colors such as black, brown, maroon, dark blue, dark green, violet, gray, and tan.

Puritan women wore a dress with a bodice with a natural waistline over a full, gathered skirt. When a tie-on collar was not worn, a large linen kerchief was folded corner to corner, draped over the shoulders, and held at the throat with a plain brooch or pin. The ensemble generally had white fold-back cuffs, which were basted to the shift. A long white apron, tucked under the bodice, was worn both indoors and out. The women wore several petticoats, and, depending on the weather, a cotton or linen shift (for housework the shift alone was enough). Large, hooded woolen cloaks were worn outdoors in inclement weather. Puritan housewives wore a girdle of ribbon or small chain around the waist with the ends hanging down to about mid-thigh. On the ends were attached household tools such as scissors, a knife, keys, a small purse, etc. Most Puritan women pulled their hair back into tight buns, over which they wore small, fitted caps for indoors. Outdoors they wore the large-brim, high-crowned hat over the cap. There was great demand for scarlet woolen material, which was made into petticoats, hoods, and cloaks. None but the most fanatic thought it irreligious to wear scarlet, and even Oliver Cromwell and the Parliamentary army wore bright red sashes over their somber-colored garb.

The Restoration Period in England (1660–1685), under Charles II, saw a determination to put the severity of Puritan fashions aside. Charles II had spent his youth in exile in the Dutch court and the French court of Louis XIV, and he and his courtiers brought back a taste for the excesses of French fashion. Rich fabrics, lace, and brightly colored ribbons were used in abundance, adorning just about any surface that would hold them. Puritan formality and starchiness gave way to studied disorder and a look of rich negligence. English Restoration fashions and the fashions of the court of Louis XIV (described below) were almost interchangeable. Charles II did produce a style of his own, introducing the long vest worn with an equally long coat, in what was called the "Persian" manner. The coat and vest were of the same fabric and color, a forerunner to today's business suit.

The final chapter on the Puritan movement began in 1620, when an English "separatist" faction that wanted to worship outside of the established Anglican Church obtained permission to start a new English settlement in the New World. Because of their long journey they were also known as "Pilgrims." They brought with them their strict rules about the "playne" dress that has been our idea of the Puritan look ever since. As is the way of the world, prosperity in the New World began to erode that ideal.

COLONIAL AND EARLY AMERICAN
The age of European colonialism began in 1492 with the arrival of Europeans in the region that we know today as the Americas. Portugal created colonies in South America; Spain established its presence primarily in Mexico, Florida, and Southern California.

In 1624, the Dutch West India Company founded New Amsterdam, a settlement that encompassed the area now known as Manhattan. It ran along the Hudson River, north to Albany. With the best harbor in North America, New Amsterdam attracted settlers from England, France, Scandinavia, Ireland, and Germany. The English took possession of New Amsterdam in 1674, changing the name to New York.

The original American colonies, Virginia (1602), Plymouth (1620), and Massachusetts Bay (1630), were first populated by religious dissenters. Carolina colonies were founded in 1630; Georgia, the last of the original thirteen colonies, was established in 1732. The English were later joined by the French, Germans, Scots, Irish, Danes, and Swiss. By 1763, several cities had developed, including New York, Boston, Philadelphia, Baltimore, and Charleston.

The French established New France in Canada in 1663, using it as a base from which to explore the Mississippi River. Claiming the land now known as Louisiana, in 1718 they established the city of New Orleans.

When the English took possession of New Amsterdam and its environs, the wealthy Dutch inhabitants were influenced by English fashions, ushering in the beginning of a unique American colonial look, which would eventually borrow from many European sources. By 1700, the greatest influence in colonial fashion was England, with most colonials, from Massachusetts to Virginia, ordering clothing, fabrics, pattern books, and furnishing from the "mother country."

BAROQUE AND ROCOCO
The reign of Louis XIV (1638–1715), the Sun King, established France as the international arbiter of style. Louis turned his quest for glory and love of conspicuous adornment into a highly profitable state business. Along with his minister of finance, Jean-Baptiste Colbert, Louis set out to dominate the European market through expanded production of luxury goods. He converted Versailles, a modest hunting lodge, into a Baroque palace, housing not only his government, but also his courtiers, who could not renew royal leases or have business with the king unless they resided at the palace.

The development of Baroque fashions during the reign of Louis XIV can be divided into three periods. The first—from about 1644 to 1660—was one of transition from the existing "cavalier" style, consisting of a jerkin (close-fitting upper-body garment) with lace trim on collar and cuffs; pantaloons; a large "falling" band collar; an ostrich-plumed hat with braid trim; and wide-cuffed riding boots or shoes decorated with ribbon rosettes. Men's hats were broad brimmed with a low, sloping crown.

Louis XIV had a full head of black hair, and men who were not so fortunate adopted wigs to ape his appearance.

To accommodate the wigs, shirt collars were reduced to neckbands with a falling lace ruffle or *jabot,* filling the jacket opening. Lace ruffles called *cannons* were worn just below the knees. The woman's costume featured a wide lingerie collar, corseted bodice, puffed sleeves, and moderately hooped gown. The already tight bodice grew tighter; sleeves moved up to three-quarter length; and necklines dropped. Under the full skirt was a bell-shaped hoop of moderate dimension. Hairstyles featured short curls over the forehead and side curls hanging to the shoulders.

During the second Baroque period (ca. 1660–1670), which was concurrent with the English Restoration, the king's satin and lace mills, and other manufacturers of fashion goods, were making France wealthy. A single costume in Baroque style might be embellished with hundreds of yards of ribbon, lace, and *passementerie* (fancy woven edging). Most popular for men during this period were petticoat, or *Rhinegrave,* breeches. These could be made either like a kilt, worn over full knee-length slops, or like extra-wide, full-cut short pants worn over loose knee breeches. The Rhinegraves were lavishly ornamented with *galloon*—lace, embroidery, or braid trim—and ribbon loops. Square-toed, high-heeled shoes were preferred to boots. Women's costume took on extravagant ornamentation with gold and silver passementerie, lace, and ribbons. Skirts were long and full, with the overskirt, or *manteau,* looped back and held by ribbon bows. The long, slim, pointed bodice over a tight, high corset persisted, and the *stomacher* (a stiffened piece fastening over the front closure or the corset) remained an essential part of the wardrobe. Sleeves were now three-quarter or elbow length, and puffs were interspersed with lace flounces. Slippers had pointed, turned-up toes and very high heels. A market developed for costume jewelry.

The third period of Baroque fashions (ca. 1670–1715) saw a great change in masculine fashions. The *doublet,* a close-fitting jacket, became a vest or waistcoat; the *justaucorps* (jacket) became a coat. Buttonholes with braid trim were called *brandenburgs.* Petticoat breeches remained fashionable until about 1680, when they were replaced by full knickerbockers. By the 1690s, closely fitted knee-length breeches that buttoned or buckled at the knee became standard. In the 1690s a scarf called a *steinkirk* replaced the jabot. The steinkirk was loosely tied around the neck in the manner of a cravat, its ends twisted and tucked into a buttonhole. Wigs grew larger, becoming more artificial in appearance, and were powdered. Around 1670, the wide, cocked-brim hat came into vogue, followed by the three-cornered hat around 1690. Both men and women painted their lips, lined their eyes, and powdered their faces. From about 1675, the hair was dressed high off the forehead in clusters of curls arranged over a silk-covered wire frame called a *commode.* High-heeled slippers called *pantouffles* were made of exquisite embroidered fabrics. Around 1650, Jaquin of Paris perfected the manufacture of artificial pearls, and a band of pearls around the neck became a fashion necessity.

Baroque's heavy grandiloquence neared its end with the death of Louis XIV; it was replaced during the reign of his great-grandson, Louis XV, by the Rococo style of exquisite refinement.

There were two Rococo periods—the first from about 1724 to 1750, the second from 1750 to 1770—during which design became less flamboyant and more dignified. The male *habit à la française* (French suit) retained the three fundamentals of coat, vest, and breeches from the Baroque period. Fabrics used to make men's suits included silks, velvets, and woolens. The heels of men's shoes were lowered; in the 1770s large square buckles were the rage. The Rococo wig became smaller and straighter and was brushed up off the forehead with a soft roll of curls called "pigeon's wings" on the sides of the face. About 1755 these wings were replaced by horizontally arranged rolls over the ears—the *cadogan* style. White wigs were the most desirable; if white was unaffordable, the wig was powdered with flour. The hat of the period was the *tricorne*—a three-cornered, or cocked, hat—edged with braid, and, perhaps, ostrich feathers.

Women's costume displayed two distinctive Rococo styles. In the early period, the Watteau gown, named after the painter, was the principal mode. The original Watteau gown was a loose sack or dress worn over a tight bodice and very full underskirt, sometimes incorporating a low, circular hoop. In the 1740s the *pagoda* sleeve took hold; it was tight from shoulder to elbow, where it spread into flared ruffles over cascading flounces of lace and ribbon. At mid-century the Watteau gown had evolved into the classic *robe à la française.* By the 1770s this style had become the formal dress for court functions, as well as the formal dress of choice in colonial America, England, and the western world. This dress had six box pleats in back stitched flat across the shoulders, and falling into a train. *Panniers* (side hoops) returned with the *robe à la française.* Extremely broad panniers on which the arms could rest were called elbow panniers; very small hoops, for morning wear, were called "considerations." Fabrics became daintier and lighter—lustrous satins and damasks, lawns, and dimities—in a variety of pastel stripes and florals.

Hair was simply dressed, pulled back into a French twist ending in a curled topknot and giving the appearance of a small head atop a voluminous gown. From the 1760s, hairdos began to increase in height. Paint and powder were applied quite freely, but in more subtle shades than in the Baroque period. Scent was freely used; baths were still considered a medical treatment and were generally avoided. A German jeweler named Strasser invented "paste" jewels, or *strass,* and suddenly all was aglitter with sparkling stones.

Marie Antoinette and Louis XIV (Louis XV's grandson) reigned from 1774 to 1792, when the House of Bourbon fell in the French Revolution and they both were beheaded. In their reign the excesses of fashion continued in a seemingly frivolous and mindless pursuit of fashion one-upmanship. Layered onto the already excessive fashions of Louis XV, hairdresses grew higher, panniers wider, and laces and trims became even more elaborate. Excessively high hairdos became conversation pieces in the France of Marie Antoinette and often displayed elaborate jokes. The frames supporting the hair, plus the weight of the "confection," generally limited the wearing of the "do" for a limited appearance before the lady had to retire. It is said that all the flour that was used for powdering the hair of Louis XIV's court could have fed France's starving peasants, and thus prevented the revolution.

GEORGIAN

In Georgian England (named after George III) during the period of Marie Antoinette's reign in France, fashions were developing along simpler lines. The English royalty seemed to prefer country life to that of the court, and an elegant country squire look developed, which though rich in fabrics, was simpler in line. Padding for fullness of the skirts replaced the panniers, hairdos were much simpler, and laces and sheer shawls gave a softer, filmier look. Artists such as Joshua Reynolds and Thomas Gainsborough glorified this pastoral look. The period was often referred to in England as the "Age of Elegance."

By the 1780s, intellectuals throughout the civilized world were becoming more interested in scientific studies and an interest in philosophy was developing, thus giving this period the sobriquet of "The Age of Reason." Women's gowns were of softer fabrics and the bosoms of the low-cut gowns were filled with a gauzy fichu or "modesty," thus giving a "pouter pigeon" look to the wearer. Hairstyles were looser, much wider, and fell to the shoulders in an artfully casual manner. Outsized broad-brimmed hats, decorated with plumes, gave the English pastoral look. The English country squire's garb of long frock coat and vest worn with knee pants and hose had little trim except the brass buttons and shoe buckles. His hair was worn natural or lightly powdered and generally pulled back into a queue, cadogan, or ponytail.

In France, Marie Antoinette, playing milkmaid at Malmaision, adapted her own version of the pastoral look.

DIRECTOIRE AND EMPIRE

The Empire period encompasses dress styles, furniture designs, and interior decoration popular in early nineteenth-century France, especially those favored by Napoleon and Empress Josephine during the First Empire (1804–1814). Napoleon's interest in ancient Rome, Greece, and Egypt stimulated creativity in direct imitation of classical styles. Empire styles spread from France to the rest of Europe, including its colonial possessions. The First Empire was preceded by the Directoire—the government of France from 1795 to 1799. This era also drew upon classical styles.

In the years leading up to the French Revolution of 1789, fashions had already begun to change to simpler designs, with less class distinction being shown, for to display elegance in public was to put one's life in jeopardy. With the fall of the French monarchy and the executions of Louis XVI and Marie Antoinette and most of their court, magnificence in dress virtually vanished.

The fundamentals of the modern male costume date from the French Revolution, when knee breeches gave way to trousers. The revolutionary street fighters who adopted the workingman's long-legged pants, were called *sans culottes*—meaning "without breeches"—the apparel of the aristocrats. Men wore knee-high "jockey" or "top" boots, generally of black leather with tan turned-down cuffs. Around 1792, the Muscadines emerged. *Muscadine* was a term of derision for flamboyantly dressed, effeminate patriotic dandies who used musk scent, reminiscent of Muscadine candies. The Muscadines were succeeded by the Incroyables (literally "incredibles"), young dandies who fitted themselves out in coats nipped at the waist and flared in the skirt, waistcoats of contrasting-colored satin, and full sheer cambric cravats. Breeches finished with ribbon loops ended below the knee. Blue and white or green and white were the preferred color combinations. Men wore their hair cropped on top and long over the ears in a style called "dogs' ears." The more elegant man of the period wore a frock coat, preferably in brown, with a black or violet collar and canary yellow or bottle green breeches. The waistcoat was dark satin, and the cravat white muslin or green, black, or scarlet silk.

Women's costume also took on a simplicity of style, with a tightly fitted bodice emphasizing the bosom. Sleeves were long and fitted; skirts were full, gathered at the waist, and worn over petticoats in lieu of hoops. A soft, full-cut lingerie gown, the *chemise à l'anglaise* (English gown), belted high with a crushed satin sash, was worn year-round. Peasants, working women, and female revolutionaries generally wore their skirts shortened to midcalf. High heels, linked to the aristocracy, were replaced by soft satin or kid flat slippers.

The elegantly dressed women's gowns of the Directoire period are of interest because, for the first time, the creators of fashion deliberately turned back to another period's clothing for inspiration—in this case, classical Greece and Rome. Designers erroneously assumed that the aged and sun-bleached ruins had always been white; therefore, white became the preferred, predominant hue in interiors and fabrics. Even a pale complexion was preferred during the Directoire and First Empire periods. The elegant result of this return to the classical past was a sheath or chemise gown, worn slightly full over a low-cut bosom, and sashed or tied just below the breast line, with the skirt usually ending in a train. Tunics were worn over the long, straight gowns, which had side slits to reveal the legs. Regardless of the season, sheer materials were used for these gowns, bringing on an epidemic of respiratory ailments, sometimes called "muslin disease," in 1803. The Incroyable's female counterpart was the Merveilleuse ("marvelous one"), who carried the classical Greek style to extremes, wearing pink silk body tights under sheer, skimpy muslin dresses, even wetting the dress to make it cling. Tiny sandals with crisscross lacing up to the knee were popular.

The revealing nature of Directoire fashions left no room for pockets, so women began carrying small drawstring reticules (purses). As for hairstyles, a classic coiffure with the psyche knot (hair knotted at the back of the head) was adapted from classic Greek sculptures. This could be decorated with combs, coronets, and nets. Hairpieces were used to produce ringlets and chignons. These were followed by various bobs, such as the Titus or Brutus styles for men and women. The Titus was cut short in layers and brushed up and out from the crown of the head, the uneven ends hanging over the forehead and ears. The Brutus was a little less shaggy, and the bangs lay flatter.

Napoleon Bonaparte, France's brilliant military hero, became First Consul in 1799 and Emperor in 1804. As Napoleon's Empire period progressed, pantaloons or trousers became an important feature of men's attire, and between 1810 and 1815, tight-fitting trousers and gaiters in a single garment became the mode. The *habit,* or suit, with trousers (generally with stirrup straps) and a coat of the same fabric became a popular item in dark blues, greens, and browns. Full dress at court and for public balls consisted of a velvet coat, black satin breeches, an elaborately embroidered silk waistcoat, a shirt with frilled wrist ruffles, a jabot or neck frill, and a neck cloth. For winter wear there were two styles of greatcoats—the *redingote,* a three-quarter or full-length coat of dress, and the *carrick,* a garment with several shoulder capes.

During the Empire period, a fashionable women's style

was the lingerie chemise gown with long sleeves divided into several puffs by narrow bands of ribbon (mamelukes). A frilly neck ruff, the *cherusse* (know as the "Betsie" in England), was popular. Another highly popular item was the *spencer,* a very short bolero jacket edged in fur, swansdown, or fringe; it originated in England, but the French quickly adapted it for both men and women. By the middle of the Empire period, the redingote became the vogue for women's winter wear. It generally had several layered shoulder capes like the men's carrick coat, but was belted high beneath the bosom to follow the Empire line. Around 1808, a high-waisted, fur-lined woman's coat appeared—the *witzchoura.*

Empress Josephine established two styles of court gown, the "little costume" and the "grand costume." The first was of embroidered satin (blue was Josephine's favorite color) with short puffed sleeves and a train falling from the belt line. The grand gown, designed in brocade with metallic threads, had long, tight sleeves and a sumptuous train falling from the left shoulder. Both gowns had square necklines with standing lace collars and were elaborately embroidered in silk, pearls, and spangles. An accessory of great importance during this period, remaining in fashion for over a century, was the cashmere paisley shawl. This fashion dates from Napoleon's Egyptian campaign, which also was responsible for the introduction of elegant turbans. Headgear in general was ornamented with ribbons, flowers, plumes, and lace.

ROMANTIC PERIOD
After the fall of Napoleon in 1816, Europe longed for the stability that had been lost with the French Revolution and the growing industrialization brought about by technological advances. Emphasis on emotion and sentiment replaced the rationalism of the earlier period and a new romanticism spread across Europe. In fashion this romanticism was reflected in a rounded silhouette for both men and women.

For women, the waist shifted from just below the bosom to just above the waist, the skirt became fuller and shorter, sleeves became fuller, and ruffles and bows made a reappearance. Hairdos were more elaborate with a profusion of curls at the temple. Women, believed to be more emotional than men, were idealized, but at the same time, were seen as weak and in need of protection. This was reflected in the doll-like silhouette of the time with its sloped shoulders, tiny waist, and full skirt.

Men's fashion exhibited a fullness as well, with a nipped-in waist, wide shoulders, and fuller trousers.

VICTORIAN
The Victorian era takes its name from the reign of Victoria, queen of England and Ireland and empress of India. Victoria was born in 1819 and ascended the throne in 1837, ruling until her death in 1901. Great Britain was at peace during most of her reign, enabling her to concentrate on trade and industry and on doubling the size of the empire.

In 1840, Victoria married her cousin, Prince Albert of Saxe-Coburg, with whom she was deeply in love. The couple had a total of nine children—four sons and five daughters. Through the marriage of her children, Victoria was related to most of the royal houses of Europe.

After the 1861 death of Prince Albert, Queen Victoria plunged into deep mourning and withdrew from public life.

Her daughters and their husbands became the trendsetters in English fashion, particularly Edward, the Prince of Wales, and his wife, Alexandra, who were the heirs apparent to the throne.

In the 1830s, Victoria dressed according to the trends of the day. In 1840, when she married Prince Albert, his style immediately began to influence her, and ultimately, all of England. Soon, Queen Victoria's clothing had become more restrained, her skirt lengths dropping to the floor, sleeves diminishing in size, and hats and hairstyles becoming more sedate. The newer silhouette for Victoria, and for her devoted female subjects, included close-fitting bodices and long, full skirts supported by many petticoats. Women began to wear small pads, or bustles, under their skirts in the back. With fashions now designed to promote the look of respectability, the shawl and poke bonnet became "de rigueur." While the shapes of women's gowns became more discreet, fashion increasingly took on more and richer decoration, often to the point of excess.

Mid-Victorian-era fashion was dominated by the crinoline. Originally a horsehair-stiffened underskirt intended to extend the bell-shaped skirt to a dome or fan shape, by the mid-1850s, the crinoline had become a cage of steel wire hoops, increasing in diameter to the bottom of the skirt, connected by tapes or curved steel ribs. With a crinoline underneath, a woman's skirt could measure up to eighteen feet around the hem. However, crinolines did eliminate the need for multiple layers of petticoats, and were thus lighter and cooler for the wearer.

Only at evening events was it socially acceptable for a lady to bare her neck, shoulders, and upper bosom, and it was considered scandalous to reveal an ankle or leg. The only time that a lady was permitted to expose her arms was on formal occasions, and then she usually wore long, fitted gloves or a wrap. Ladies were expected to wear gloves, indoors or out, at all times, except when dining. Silk, the prevailing fabric, ran the gamut from light summer sheer, to heavier silk satin, to heaviest velvet. Pastel colors were in style, for day or evening.

By the 1860s, skirts were slimmed down below the waist by means of gores rather than gathers, and the princess cut was lending a funnel, rather than a dome, shape to skirts, even though the diameter of the hem remained huge. Also during the 1860s the bonnet began its decline, and smaller—even brimless—hats came into vogue. For the first time in twenty years, the back of the neck could be seen, and the use of elaborate and voluminous artificial hairpieces became quite popular. By the late '60s, the shorter walking dress, with a hem above the ankle held up by ties, was favored for women's outdoor excursions.

The fashions and illustrations of the late Victorian period glorified femininity, exemplified by cinched waists and full-hipped silhouettes. By the 1870s the crinoline was losing ground, and the interest in women's silhouettes was shifting to the back via the bustle. Initially, the shape was still full—with only the overskirt being pulled to the rear to form the bustle; but by the end of the decade the skirt was becoming more vertical, with an elaborate bustle generally ending in a train. Both the popular cuirasse bodice—a very tight, boned outer garment extending from chest to hip, intended to mold the body—and the princess sheath imparted a slimming appearance to women to the hip level.

In the late 1870s, many intellectuals turned away from conventional fashion and adopted Pre-Raphaelite style dress in their desire to return to the simple, unconstrained cut of early medieval gowns.

There were other styles outside of the accepted, orthodox fashions that would eventually leave their mark on fashion history. One of these came from Alma Jenks Bloomer of Homer, New York. She edited a ladies' magazine, the "Lily" (1848–1854), that was dedicated to women's rights and temperance. She created and adopted the full trousers, worn under shortened skirts, as a means of freeing women for less restricted movement than that allowed by the conventional styles of the period. She also eschewed the tiny-waisted corset for a more natural waistline. She called her movement "Rational Dress."

Throughout the '80s, the bustle remained constant, although the skirt generally became less voluminous. All sorts of devices were invented to support the weight of the bustle, including frames of wire, horsehair, wicker, and even steel springs. Special furniture had to be invented to accommodate the bustle. The "fainting bench" was a chair with one armrest that enabled a woman to sit sidesaddle, sparing her bustle from being crushed. Finally, by the 1890s, the bustle had virtually disappeared in favor of the princess line with gored skirts; the gores were cut fuller in the back to form a train, a silhouette that would remain popular until the end of the century. Fabrics of this period ranged in texture and weight from the lightest sheers to heavy, upholstery-like plushes and brocades. A wide range of color was employed, from the palest to the deepest of tones.

To be fashionably dressed in Victorian times was time consuming—no fewer than seven complete wardrobe changes per day were needed to be *comme il faut.* A lady's numerous complete changes of dress per day included a morning dressing gown, a riding outfit, a luncheon dress, a day or walking dress, a visiting gown for afternoon calls, a smart outfit for carriage rides through the park, a dinner gown, and an elegant evening gown. Since a true leader of the social set could not be seen twice in the same ensemble during the same week, or indeed in subsequent weeks if she were truly in the limelight, the basic wardrobe could be multiplied enormously, requiring daily fittings by one's own dressmaker as well as regular visits to the couturier for a new "look" each season.

At the beginning of the Victorian era, men of fashion seemed as determined as women to cover themselves so that only their faces were exposed. Paragons of style were expected to change their gloves at least seven times a day. A gentleman required seven coats: four morning coats, a frock coat for formal occasions, a dress tailcoat for evening, and an overcoat. Daytime coats were generally dark brown, dark green, navy, or deep purple. For evening, men often wore black and deep blue with white shirts and ties. Styles of men's coats included the "Prince Albert," a double-breasted, knee-length frock coat; the sack coat, with its finger-length sleeves and straight-cut body; and the morning coat, similar to the sack coat but with a rounded-off skirt front. Also popular were the mid-thigh-length redingote with a nipped waist, and the claw-hammer, or swallowtail, coat.

After 1850, men's tailcoats and frock coats were reserved for formal or evening wear. The dinner coat, known in the United States as the "Tuxedo," first appeared in the 1880s. Waistcoats were made of colorful embroidered or brocade fabric. From season to season, there was a lot of experimentation with the size and cut of men's coats, especially the lapels.

In the 1840s, men's trousers were tightly cut, held down with straps that passed under a man's shoes. By the 1850s, trousers were cut looser, and the foot straps disappeared. Creased trousers appeared in the 1860s, and cuffs around the turn of the century. During the day, men wore their trousers a shade paler than their coats, often in checked or plaid fabric. For evening, they tended to choose lighter-colored trousers, but dark, matching trousers and jackets were starting to become popular.

By the 1850s, more casual "country clothes" became popular, usually made in lighter colors and sturdier fabric than "town" clothes.

AMERICAN CIVIL WAR

The look of American fashion underwent a change during the decade leading up to and including the Civil War (1861–1865). With the prosperity brought on by the Industrial Revolution, it had become common for wealthy Americans to go to Europe on the "Grand Tour," returning with stylish new wardrobes from France (women) or England (men). At the same time, a considerable fashion industry was emerging in New York, for the invention of the sewing machine in 1846 had made it easier and faster for dressmakers to do their work. Many New York dressmaking firms imported French and English originals to copy and sell, or followed patterns from *Godey's Lady's Book,* a pioneering fashion magazine that interpreted the latest European styles for Americans. By the start of the Civil War, other magazines (such as *Harper's Bazar*) were founded in imitation of *Godey's,* helping to bring fashion to homes throughout America.

Like their European counterparts, American women at that time relied on tightly laced bone corsets to shape their figures; the most fashionable strove to have a fifteen-inch waist. In contrast, their full, bell-shaped skirts were made wider and wider, until by the 1860s they measured as much as ten yards around. Underneath this a woman of the early 1850s would wear long, lace-trimmed white muslin drawers, a crinoline or petticoat of calico (quilted and reinforced with whalebone), and several starched muslin petticoats with flounces; in winter there might be an additional flannel petticoat. During the mid-fifties the multiple petticoats were replaced by the cage crinoline. By 1860 the predominance of the crinoline and the bell-shaped skirt was already in decline.

Gowns and wraps were lavishly decorated with embroidery, galloon, silk or woolen lace, braid, frogs, tassels, fringe, ribbon, or passementerie. Formal gowns were made of such fabrics as brocade, heavy satin, silk, moiré, and, most popular of all, taffeta. Ball gowns were of gauze, tulle, tarlatan, or lace, while day dresses might be of fine wool, alpaca, mohair, velveteen, or foulard. Summer dresses favored linen, cambric, muslin, piqué, and batiste. Lace mitts, soft gloves, parasols, and pouch bags were popular accessories. By the beginning of the Civil War, the customary bonnet had been generally replaced by a small hat worn forward, a style introduced by Empress Eugénie of France. Hair was worn neatly parted in the center and drawn back into a bun, or in a snood made of string, ribbon, or human hair; in the evening this was often ornamented.

The most common colors for daytime clothing were soft browns, olive, amber, and vanilla, although the more formal gowns and cloaks might use deep greens, wines, violets, and blues: by far the most popular color for ball gowns was white, usually trimmed in pastel colors. Brown silk paired with black velvet was a popular combination, and stripes of all widths were much in fashion. Scottish plaids were highly fashionable for both women and children, and young boys often wore kilts.

At the start of the Civil War, both sides expected the conflict to be resolved quickly and did not prepare for the privation that war brings. The fighting dragged on, however, and as supplies ran low, the industrial North proved to have the advantage, especially in the production of military clothing. Most of the fabric mills were in the North, and there, too, a new machine for sewing leather made possible the mass production of boots, a real advantage for a marching army. (A disadvantage was that the Union's mass-produced uniforms were often ill-fitting, and many soldiers spent their off-hours altering their clothing by hand.) The less fortunate Confederate soldier, once his first uniform had worn out, was often forced to salvage clothing and boots from corpses on the field after a battle. Many Southern women disassembled their own wardrobes, using the material to make shirts, trousers, and underwear for the men at the front. Fashion came to a near standstill in the South after 1863; in the North the difference was less noticeable, for even with the South blockaded, cotton for fabrics could be imported from India and other parts of the world.

EDWARDIAN

The Edwardian period of fashion began about 1880. By that time Queen Victoria's influence on fashion had waned, and her son, Edward, the Prince of Wales, and his wife, Alexandra, became the world's fashion leaders. Edwardian society molded itself to the king's personal demands. Everything was larger than life, with an avalanche of balls, dinners, and weekend-long country house parties. More money was spent on clothes, food, horse racing, hunting parties, yachting, and dalliances than ever before. High fashion was a badge of social status, and its devotees regarded it with great seriousness and full absorption. Perhaps the most apt description of the era would be "extravagant opulence." Edward saw himself as fashion's leader, and both he and Alexandra paid great attention to, and devoted much time to their dress.

Being at the height of fashion meant great formality and immense luxury in clothes, and required wearing the "correct" clothes on all occasions. A fashionable lady would change her dress and accessories five or six times a day, and would avoid wearing an ensemble that had been seen before. Queen Alexandra was the apex of fashion, and her favorite designers were Redfern of London, and Doucet, Fromont, and Worth of Paris. Other fashionable Parisian couturiers were Paquin, Cheruit, and Doeuillet.

Although the era bore Edward's name, it was feminine fashion that distinguished it. The ideal in feminine beauty was a full, mature figure with a generous "pouter pigeon" bosom. Although emphasis was on a large (often enhanced) bosom, cleavage was taboo.

The last two decades of the nineteenth century saw hints of the coming women's liberation with swimming costumes that had long bloomers, leading to "Moorish" trousers under a knee-length tunic worn for tennis. Even lady bicyclists wore knickerbockers. But all were properly corseted underneath. Often the only thing that made a costume sportive was the hat. For boating, sailor hats were the vogue; for tennis, a straw skimmer was the thing.

By the turn of the twentieth century, the bustle had been forgotten, skirts flared out below the knee and reached the ground, jackets were mannish with squared full shoulders and tight sleeves, and high collars were the rage. Even with low-cut evening wear, the jeweled dog collar, introduced by Alexandra, was worn to cover the neck.

Lingerie and petticoats were of silk in delicate colors, and were lavishly ornamented with embroidery and lace. Winter dresses were made of velvet, satin, poplin, damask, serge, and brocade. Summer fabrics included light silks, foulard, muslin, tulle, and lace.

Alexandra introduced curled "fringe" bangs (often false hair on a band so that the lady did not have to cut her own tresses). By the turn of the century the pompadour style of hairdo with a psyche knot of top was "in," although the fringe was still incorporated.

Men's fashions became more standardized as the period progressed, with the Saville Row tailor acting as high priest. The morning coat was the most usual formal daytime wear. The shirt was usually cotton and generally lightly starched; it had a detachable collar that was always stiffly starched. The shirt collar could be turned down for day wear, but was always worn standing up for the evening. Vests, or waistcoats, as they were more popularly known, were essential to every suit. For day wear, a heavy gold watch was worn in one pocket, the fob in an opposite pocket, with the chain draped across the front of the waistcoat. Evening suits were of vicuña or worsted. At this time the less formal dinner jacket was introduced, but it could not be worn for formal occasions or when ladies were present, being reserved for informal suppers, a night on the town, or the music halls. Suits for day and formal wear were generally dark blue or black, with lighter tans or checks worn for country or leisure wear. Many men wore a corset to control their figure, although one wonders why, since suits were very bulky in cut, requiring five yards of fabric for the average man. The body of the suit was made to appear even more bulky via small, high-button collars and short lapels. By the turn of the century, trousers were being cut in the peg-top mode—full and pleated at the waist with legs that tapered to a tight fit at the ankle. By 1900, trouser cuffs were being seen, a result of men turning up the bottoms of their pants when at the races to keep them from getting spattered by mud. In hats, the silk topper was the most formal, with the bowler or derby a bit less dressy. The deerstalker and Alpine hats were popular for country wear. There were a variety of caps, particularly the new motoring caps of hard finished cotton. Edward introduced the German soft Homburg, or fedora, hat as an alternative to the hard bowler, or derby. Sleeping pajamas of Oriental origin were introduced in the 1880s as an alternative to the nightshirt.

The Edwardian era was the last period in fashion when the impetus for new trends came exclusively from the ruling class, in this case the Prince and Princess of Wales (later the king and queen). New methods of manufacture, scientific advances, technology, and changes in social and economic matters were leading to the shifting of fashion from high society to the masses, especially in the United States. Comfort and freedom of movement would soon replace Edwardian formality and opulence.

ABOUT THE ILLUSTRATIONS

001. Man and women of the mercantile class, England, ca. 1600. These Londoners are wearing small ruffs to accessorize their modest clothing. The women's gowns have short, puffed sleeves and have lost the farthingale and bum roll foundations. The man's coat features long, hanging sleeves trimmed in fur.

002. James I of England and his queen, Anne of Denmark, ca. 1610. The monarch wears a doublet with falling-band collar, a jeweled cape, and paned, jewel-studded trunk hose over knee-length canions with ribbon garters. Hose and slip-on shoes with decorative shoe roses complete the outfit. James's queen is wearing a richly patterned silk gown decorated with a high standing collar and intricate lace cuffs. The dress is worn over a French wheel farthingale (which took its name from its cylindrical shape) reinforced with spokes.

003. King Henry IV of France and his queen, Marie de Médicis, in formal court dress, ca. 1610. Henry wears a buttoned, fitted doublet with a short peplum and epaulets at the arm scythe. His paned trunk hose are of the same brocaded satin as the doublet. He wears silk stockings, shoes with large ribbon shoe roses, and a hat with a wire-frame crown. The queen wears a corseted doublet with expanded wings and a gathered peplum over her farthingale-styled skirt. Her sleeves are padded and end in lace-edged cuffs. A padded satin crown finishes her outfit.

004. Jamestown settlers with a Native American, ca. 1607. Named after the king of England, Jamestown was the first British settlement in the New World, occupied mainly by the military. Native American, left, in loincloth and beads. A musket man, center, wearing chain mail, wide breeches, and high, cuffed boots. A commanding officer, right, dressed in a jerkin and trunk hose, with a ruff at his neck and knees.

005. King Henry IV of France, Marie de Médicis, and their son, Louis (later Louis XIII), ca. 1610. The French king wears a small ruff, doublet, and Spanish slops over knitted hose and shoes with lace shoe roses. Dutch slops (also called German plunderhosen) are similar, but fall below the knee.

006. English royal children, ca. 1610. Dressed in the style of her elders, the princess wears a striped silk gown with a wheel farthingale and a standing lace whisk. The boy wears a braid-trimmed gown with a falling ruff. He holds early versions of a golf club and golf ball.

007. Dutch aristocrats in court dress, ca. 1620. In 1609 Holland gained her freedom from Spain through treaty, becoming a parliamentary monarchy. Dutch aristocracy still looked to France for fashion while the French looked to Spain. This couple is dressed in the "Spanish mode," which gave prominence to dark, somber colors. White cuffs and collars.

008. Pilgrim farm couple in North America. ca. 1610. Jamestown was the first permanent English settlement in North America, established in 1607. Its leaders were military and generally of the nobility, but its actual settlers were from the lower class of farmers, who often had Puritan leanings.

009. English gentlemen, ca. 1614–16. This elegantly dressed man, left, wears a flowered silk doublet with a lace whisk collar and a scalloped gorget. His brocade Spanish slops are fastened with points tied in bowknots pulled through the peplum at the waist. One of his boots is turned down to expose his knit stocking. This gentleman, right, models a doublet edged with gimp, with sleeves to match. His slops are embroidered with a celestial pattern, and are worn over silk stockings and shoes with lace shoe roses.

010. English upper-middle-class family, ca. 1620. This young family is dressed in its finest. The father wears a *gullila*, or Spanish-styled starched collar, and a shirt with a lace-trimmed bib front. The outfit is completed with a short-sleeved jacket and Venetians. The mother's bodice has attached short sleeves over longer lingerie sleeves with triple lace cuffs. She wears a falling ruff at the neck. The seated child wears a scalloped triple ruff, and the other wears a lace whisk. At this period, small boys and girls were dressed alike in loose gowns.

011. English and Dutch gentleman at court, ca. 1620. The Englishman, left, wears an ensemble of doublet and slops of brocaded satin that match the lining of his velvet cape. His full slops became known as Venetians. The Dutch gentleman, right, is similarly garbed, with the exception of wearing a wired whisk in lieu of a pleated ruff. He wears a broad-brimmed beaver hat with plumes.

012. French court clothes, ca. 1620. The lady wears a ribbon-trimmed taffeta bodice and sleeves, and a solid taffeta overskirt pinned up to reveal a brocaded underskirt. She carries a matching fabric muff with fur trim. Her collar is of lingerie fabric, sewn with tucks for shape and stiffening. The gentleman wears a slashed, buttoned doublet with epaulets. His sleeves are paned, as are his slops. He wears Russian leather scallop-topped boots over his canions.

013. King Louis XIII of France and his favorite, Charles de Luynes, ca. 1620. The king (left) and his favorite enjoying pinches of snuff, a new import from the American colonies. By this time, the "cavalier" look had developed in France. The corseted shape was discarded in favor of a waistcoat with sleeves, and the ruff had been replaced by a falling band edged with lace. The waistcoat's sleeves were generally slashed, exposing the shirt. The shirt gained visibility because the waistcoat was often left open in the back, and the lower buttons left unfastened in front. The king's cloak is trimmed with gold galloon. It was considered impolite not to wear a cloak at this time. The bows and loops at the bottom of the breeches were now called cannons. Shorter, wide-topped, bucket-shaped boots became the vogue.

014. Dutch regent and his wife, ca. 1620–30.

015. Puritans in North America, ca. 1620.

016. Middle-class couple, France, ca. 1624. The man wears a tabbed doublet over slops, and canions with ribbon garters and hose. His cloak features the new Brandenburg style of fastening, using braid and buttons. The woman wears a leather bodice over a short-sleeved jacket, to which she has buttoned on longer sleeves. Her blouse, of lingerie fabric, has a wide tucked and stiffened collar matched by the sleeve cuffs. Her apron is tucked into the bodice.

017. "Nouveau riche" middle class, France, ca. 1625. The two ladies wear tightly corseted bodices with voluminous attached sleeves and horizontal stand-up collars, exposing much of the shoulder and collarbone. It became quite fashionable to pin up the overskirt on both sides, revealing richly made petticoats. The gentleman wears a paned doublet with a satin baldric across his chest and a silk sash around his waist. The tabbed peplum of the bodice has lengthened to almost the length of a modern suit coat. His plunderhosen, which fall below the knee, are padded for fullness, and he wears bucket-topped boots with large spur leathers. He wears a fluted falling band and has arranged a "love-lock" of his hair to drape on it.

018. English country gentry, ca. 1630. Shown in the Van Dyke–inspired version of the cavalier fashion, this gentleman wears a velvet jacket with slashed sleeves and passementerie (elaborate trim); Brandenburg closures down the front. The breeches are of a contrasting color and have a frontal closure of tied points. The decorative cannons below the knee are loops of ribbon, and his boot hose are embroidered lace. His embroidered Van Dyke collar is tied with band strings, and he carries a cloak. The lady wears a taffeta gown with a lace falling band and sleeve ruffles with a matching lace-edged fichu, held in place by points at the waist. The stomacher and corset tabs match the gown in color and fabric. A beaver hat with plumes and a love-lock finish the outfit.

019. A family of the Spanish court, ca. 1630. The mother wears a *basquine* (a stiffened bodice with flared hip-skirt). The gown has shoulder wings and bombast-padded sleeves. The boy wears a soft leather tabard over Spanish slops. His sleeves are of brocaded satin; his collar is a soft, unpleated ruff. The father wears a striped satin doublet with shoulder wings over full slops and silk hose. His shoes have a "shoe rose." He wears a knee-length *manta* (cloak) and a *valona* (flat semi-circular collar) supported by a *golilla* (wire frame). The valona superseded the ruff.

020. English theatrical costumes, ca. 1631. These elaborate costumes were designed by Inigo Jones for the court pantomime *Chlorinda* by dramatist Ben Jonson. Jones had been the court designer/decorator for James I and Queen Anne, and continued in that capacity for Charles I. He is best known for his architectural works, including the Banqueting House in London's Whitehall district.

021. French court couple in promenade dance, ca. 1625. The lady wears a tightly corseted bodice with tabs, topped with a broad, tucked and starched eyelet-lawn collar. Her sleeves are slashed to reveal satin undersleeves, and her overskirt is open in front, coat-like, to reveal a satin underskirt. On her head she wears a fine linen head-cloth. The cavalier wears his broad-brimmed beaver hat with plumes, a love-lock, and a lace-edged falling collar. His jerkin has slashed sleeves and tucked lace-edged cuffs. The band of bows at his waist are ribbon points, pulled through eyelets and tied to support his breeches. His jacket and breeches are decorated with gathered ribbon and beads. He has ribbon garters, and lace shoe roses finish his festive costume.

022. Dutch settlers in North America skating on the Hudson River, ca. 1630.

023. Dutch ladies of New Amsterdam, ca. 1630.

024. Queen Henrietta Maria and King Charles I of England, ca. 1633. Queen Henrietta, the sister of French king Louis XIII, followed the lead of French court fashions. Here she wears a taffeta gown with an embroidered eyelet lingerie falling band, and a fichu that also tapers into embroidered eyelet fabric. The cuffs of her sleeves are gathered petals of lingerie fabric. Charles wears the cavalier look as interpreted by Van Dyck. His velvet jacket contrasts with his satin breeches, and he wears knee-high boots with the tops folded into a cuff. His broad satin baldric supports his sword and he carries deeply cuffed leather gauntlets.

025. French cavaliers, ca. 1630.

026. French courtiers, ca. 1633. This courtier wears a velvet-slashed jerkin with ribbon rosettes at the waist. The jerkin is left open to show the undershirt, and the breeches closure is tied with points. He has a plain falling band held with strings, and his sleeves end in double cuffs, plain over

scalloped eyelet. His lady wears a gown of taffeta over satin sleeves, underskirt, and stomacher. Shirred ribbon trim adorns the bodice, sleeves, and underskirt. She wears a plain wide lingerie collar and deep lingerie cuffs, and tops the outfit with a knitted cap, rather like a tam pulled to the back.

027. French and English soldiers, ca. 1636. The French soldier, left, is wearing a green ribbed doublet with sleeves that emerge from his leather overtunic. He wears slashed knee-length breeches with bunched canions of the same fabric. Accessories include a wide wine-colored waist sash, leather baldric, and a neckpiece with a cross worn under his white falling band. Completing the outfit are bucket boots with butterfly spur leathers. The English soldier, right, is wearing a brown wide-brimmed beaver hat trimmed with rust-colored plumes, a embroidered falling collar, a metal breastplate worn over a long-skirted rust-colored tunic, a green fabric baldric, leather sword belt, brown leather gauntlets, and boots.

028. French cavalier and lady, ca. 1640. This cavalier wears a doublet with paned wings and deep tabs, a shirt with paned sleeves gathered into deep cuffs, and breeches with ribbon points for frontal closure and attachment to the doublet. He wears the typical bucket boots and broad-brimmed hat. The cape with a broad collar and no sleeves is called a balagnie cloak. His sword is carried in a tooled-leather baldric. The lady wears a cloth gown, tucked up at the sides to reveal a contrasting colored underskirt with gimp trim. Her falling band has double-scalloped lace edging, and her slashed sleeves reveal lawn undersleeves. She wears a sun mask for protection from the weather and carries a fur muff.

029. French egg seller and water vendor, ca. 1640. This egg seller and water vendor are wearing patched clothes that have been previously owned by others. Generally, the poorer the commoner, the older and less fashionable the clothes. Nevertheless, some of the style elements worn by the upper classes are visible here, such as the man's plumed hat, the woman's underskirt, and the full sleeves of their outfits.

030. Cavalier and Puritan, England, ca. 1645. The English cavalier, left, is dressed like the aristocratic or well-to-do man throughout the rest of Europe, in a gaily-colored silk, satin, or velvet matching jacket and breeches, decorated with braid; a lace falling band, cuffs, and boot hose tops; a cloak; plumed swashbuckler's hat; gloves; and bucket topped boots with butterfly spur shields and high heels. The Puritan wears the typical plain clothes and somber colors although his cape could be of scarlet wool.

031. Upper-middle-class Puritans, England, ca. 1645. English Protestants who were in sympathy with the Puritan and Parliamentarian cause. They have adopted most of the Puritan costume, but do not follow their rules of strict simplicity. The ladies open gown and brightly patterned underskirt would not meet strict Puritanical standards, while the man's ribbons at throat and knee would be considered frivolous.

032. Early Baroque fashions, France, ca. 1645.

033. Royalist soldiers and a farm girl, England, ca. 1642–45. A royalist militiaman, left, and pikeman, right, receive refreshment from a farm girl. The pikeman wears red and white sleeves for identification.

034. Parliamentary musketeer and pikeman, England, ca. 1642–45. The musketeer, left, is using a support fork to aid in firing his musket. From his bandolier hang gunpowder cases. His bodice and breeches are padded for protection. The pikeman, right, wears body armor and a red and black shirt.

035. Contrasting styles—common folk and aristocrat, France, ca. 1646.

036. Oliver Cromwell with a Parliamentarian and his wife, England, ca. 1646. Cromwell, left, confers with a Parliamentarian and his lady. They all wear somber-toned clothes, but Cromwell and the Parliamentarian wear red sashes as a sign of their office.

037. English Puritan common folk, ca. 1650.

038. French upper-class styles, ca. 1650.

039. Townspeople in New Amsterdam, ca. 1650.

040. Widow's costume, France, ca. 1660.

041. American Puritans, ca. 1660. Because many strict Puritans feared renewed Catholic harassment from James, they chose to leave for America to start a settlement there. This is the sort of garments the "Mayflower" pilgrims who landed on Plymouth Rock would have worn.

042. Dutch merchant-class couple, ca. 1660. A young merchant wears a version of Rhinegraves, jacket, and cloak, all stripped of excessive decoration. His lady wears a dark-toned gown with a broad white collar and lifts her skirt to reveal her red petticoat.

043. Louis XIV of France and a court lady, ca. 1660. Louis wears the French version of Rhinegraves, with a short jacket. The ladies' gown with its divided skirt and low cut neckline is the height of fashion for this time. Note her wired curls and falling tendrils.

044. Charles II of England and his sister, Mary Stuart, ca. 1660. Charles, son of the executed Charles I, spent most of his exile in the court of Louis XIV and upon his restoration to the throne of England, brought with him a taste for French fashion. Here he is seen dancing with his sister, Mary. He wears Rhinegraves and the shortened jacket both bedecked with ribbon loops and bows. Mary's gown is simple in cut and features a falling band from neck to elbow.

045. A noble and his son in Restoration England, ca. 1663. The nobleman wears Rhinegraves with a long coat *(justacorps)*. Every surface is covered with decoration: gold embroidery, lace, ribbons, and brocaded fabrics. The boy also wears Rhinegraves but with a shorter jacket and a cloak. His outfit is of brightly colored satins with multicolored ribbon loops and bows. His falling band is plain white with collar ties of gold thread.

046. Aristocratic mother and her children in Restoration England, ca. 1663. The mother is wearing a bright colored velvet bodice and skirt over a lawn chemise. Her petticoat is of a contrasting silk. A ladder of ribbons called "échelle" holds her bodice closure and the slits of her sleeves. The little girl wears a silk gown with a closed bodice and open overskirt in a light color. Her white lawn collar was called a "whisk" or "band." The little boy in the walker wears a brimmed cap over a fitted lawn cap. His short-sleeved long skirted gown is of brightly colored silk, while his band and chemise are of white lawn. Little boys wore skirts until they were about five or six.

047. Men's fashions, England, ca. 1666. About this time the Rhinegraves with the short jacket, left, fell out of favor when Charles II introduced the long coat and long vest worn over narrow knee breeches, right. He called this costume the "Persian" mode and it was soon adopted and adapted throughout the continent.

048. French peasants, seventeenth century. Throughout the century the lot and dress of the French peasant remained the same. They were the poorest of the poor, eking out an existence at the bottom of the food chain. Their clothing generally consisted of rags from the scrap bin.

049. Queen Maria Theresa of France, ca. 1670.

050. A lady of the court and King Louis XIV of France, ca. 1670.

051. A palace guard and a musketeer, France, ca. 1660–1700.

052. King Louis XIV of France, ca. 1670.

053. Wealthy Boston Pilgrim family, ca. 1674. Some English Puritans, especially from the merchant class, settled in Boston, becoming rather wealthy over the years. This young mother has strayed from the Puritan ideal, wearing pearls, lace trim on her cap, a lace collar, and appliquéd lace on her petticoat. Note the ribbons that hang from the baby's and the boy's shoulders; these were called "ribbons of childhood" and were popular on the continent and in America for a brief time. The man is dressed in more traditional Puritan mode.

054. Dutch-American couple in formal dress, ca. 1670.

055. French-American farmers, ca. 1680–1700.

056. French gentleman and lady, ca. 1680.

057. Louis XIV of France and lady, ca 1680. Louis took Charles II's rather simple "Persian" outfit and turned it into a work of splendor, layering it with gold embroidery. He combined the full-bottomed wig with it to make it the model of high fashion. The lady with him is wearing a hairstyle and cap called the "fontange." Her jacket becomes one with the manteau (overskirt) forming a train. The lace design on her skirt is called "pretintailles" meaning that it was appliquéd to the skirt.

058. Lady of the French court, ca. 1680.

059. Restoration gown and Puritan garb, England, ca. 1685. Dissention arose again between the Catholic and Protestant factions when James II became king. The fashions of neither the aristocracy nor the Parliamentarians changed much, as seen here.

060. Wealthy Anglo-American merchant couple, ca. 1685–1700.

061. Madame de Maintenon, France, ca. 1690.

062. French nobleman, ca. 1690.

063. French nobleman and his son, ca. 1690.

064. French noblewoman and her daughter, ca. 1690.

065. French gentleman and lady "at home," ca. 1690–1710.

066. Street scene, France, ca. 1700.

067. Anglo-American townspeople—laborers or artisans, ca. 1720–70.

068. Changing French styles, ca. 1725.

069. Anglo-American colonial merchant couple, ca. 1725.

070. Anglo-American colonial girls, ca. 1725–40.

071. Strolling couple, France, ca. 1725. The lady wears a silk Watteau gown, in a French adaptation of an Oriental flower print on gown and underskirt. On her powdered hair she wears a small ruffled cap with short ribbon lappets. Her shoes are embroidered silk. The gentleman's costume consists of a cloth coat with silk vest and breeches and a white shirt with a cravat and jabot. He wears a powdered bagwig with pigeon wing side curls and a cocked hat with gold braid trim.

072. Fashionable French couple, ca. 1730. The gentleman wears a brightly colored silk habit. The vest is edged with a satin band of a paler color. The lady wears a dark silk hood with a shoulder cape over her mantilla of flowered silk.

The mantilla is caught around the waist by a ribbon, the back is artfully arranged to reveal her brightly colored taffeta petticoat.

073. French gentleman and lady in latest styles, ca. 1730.

074. Watteau gown with Chinese motif, France, ca. 1740.

075. Anglo-American colonial lady, ca. 1746.

076. Anglo-American colonial lady in a formal gown, ca. 1740–50.

077. Scottish immigrants in North America, ca. 1745.

078. Robe à la Française, ca. 1750.

079. Anglo-American colonial shop girl or maid, ca. 1750–60.

080. Anglo-American colonial couple, ca. 1750–75.

081. Anglo-American colonists dancing, ca. 1750–65.

082. Virginia settlers, ca. 1760–70.

083. Colonial winter outerwear, ca. 1750–70.

084. A colonial merchant and his family, ca. 1760–70.

085. Stylish French couple, ca. 1760.

086. Madame Pompadour, France, ca. 1760.

087. Georgian gown, England, ca. 1760. A gown based on one of Gainsborough's portraits of 1760, illustrating the simpler hairdo and softer lines of the gown of the period.

088. Shepherdess style, France, ca. 1760.

089. An English officer and a colonial lady, North America, ca. 1760.

090. North-American colonial gentleman and lady, ca. 1770.

091. Rococo gown, France, ca. 1775.

092. Elaborate hairdo, court of Marie Antoinette, France, ca. 1775. Hairdo saluting the French navy with one of her battleships atop a cluster of rolling waves of hair. Her gown is called a "gown à la circassienne" and has a rounder, more balloon-like silhouette than the panniered gown. The man's habit has changed little since that of Louis XV.

093. Court of Marie Antoinette and Louis XVI, France, ca. 1776. This is an example of one of Marie Antoinette's opera ensembles which features the high powdered hairdo, made higher with ostrich plumes, and the richly decorated panniered silk gown.

094. Georgian England, "The Age of Reason," ca. 1780. This lady is wearing a day gown of a soft fabric, a gauzy fichu, and a broad-brimmed hat. The country squire is wearing a frock coat, vest, knee pants and hose. His hair is lightly powdered.

095. French adaptation of English rural fashions, ca. 1780. This drawing is based on a sketch of Marie Antoinette's adaptation of the English country look and is her dressmaker's version of dressing simply. By now, the English were adopting bigger hats and wider, looser hairdos. This trend in headwear also influenced the French fashions, as seen in this feather-bedecked turban on a wide brushed out coiffure. The gentleman's attire is also becoming simpler, with little ornamentation. He wears an American beaver hat, which has become all the rage. The general effect is almost Puritanical except that lighter, pastel colors were often preferred.

096. English "sports," ca. 1781. The two young women here were generally referred to as "sports" and were a by-product of the English gambling houses and sports clubs of the 1780s where they met English gentlemen who were seeking companionship. It was often the mode for these young women to allow their bosom to be partially exposed as a sign of their availability. Otherwise, their gowns and hairdos are in keeping with the latest modes of the gentry. The girl on the left wears a pale satin ensemble while her friend wears a gown of pastel silk layered over with brightly colored embroidered gauze.

097. British "Gainsborough" look, ca. 1785. Seen here is a later version of the "Gainsborough look," from 1785. The new vogue is for the lady's hair to be frizzed and brushed out at the sides with long rolled curls hanging around the shoulders. The broad-brimmed and ostrich-plumed hat is still in fashion and her pale toned silk gown is softened with a sheer stole, sheer fichu, and collar. The gentleman wears a claw-hammer tailed coat and carries a tricorne low-crowned beaver hat. His hair is teased out at the sides and worn in a ribboned queue at the back

098. French gentleman and lady, ca. 1789.

099. Muscadine and lady, France, ca. 1792.

100. Muscadine and lady, France, ca. 1793.

101. Sansculotte and female revolutionary, France, ca. 1793–94.

102. Revolutionary street fighters, France, ca. 1793–94.

103. Soldiers of the Directoire and First Empire, France, ca. 1795. Hussar (cavalryman), left, wears braided waistcoat and short braided jacket with fur trim. His green uniform has silk braid and gold button; black hat has red band and green plume. Officer of the Light Infantry, center, wears cutaway jacket and long waistcoat; blue tailcoat with red revers, collar with brass buttons; white waistcoat and breeches; black plumed hat. Line cavalryman, right, wears a blue jacket, a red-lined tailcoat with golden revers, white bandoleer (shoulder band), and black tan-cuffed boots.

104. Soldiers, France, ca. 1795. Infantryman, left, in blue jacket with red revers, collar, cuffs, and epaulettes; white waistcoat and red-, white-, and blue-striped pants; white spats and black shoes; black hat. Musketeer, center, wears a white jacket with rust-red revers; white waistcoat, pants, and bandoleer; black gaiters. His brass and black leather helmet sports a black plume. Line infantryman, right, wears blue coat with red revers, epaulettes, and collar; white waistcoat and pants with black gaiters; black bicorne (two-cornered) hat with flowering red plume.

105. Merchant and his daughters, France, ca. 1795.

106. Merchant's wife and son, France, ca. 1795.

107. Incroyables, France, ca. 1796.

108. Merveilleuses, France, ca. 1796.

109. Dance costumes, France, ca. 1796.

110. Dance costumes, France, ca. 1796.

111. Vendeuse and merchant, France, ca. 1796.

112. Member of Directoire and lady, France, ca. 1799.

113. Napoleon Bonaparte, France, ca. 1800.

114. Gentleman and lady of the First Empire, France, ca. 1800.

115. French couple in walking costumes, ca. 1800.

116. A well-dressed French couple, ca. 1800.

117. Mother and daughters, France, ca. 1800.

118. Two stylish French women, ca. 1802.

119. Evening wear, France, ca. 1803.

120. French gentleman and lady, ca. 1804.

121. Coronation of Empress Josephine, France, ca. 1804.

122. Napoleon Bonaparte, France, ca. 1804.

123. Emperor Napoleon Bonaparte and Empress Josephine, France, ca. 1804.

124. American Quakers, ca. 1804. The American Quaker's mode of dress, while never considered "stylish" was a quiet influence on fashions, both at home and abroad. Their preference for simple, unadorned garb, helped diminish fashion's fussiness. The Quakers generally preferred pale gray, blue, or pink colors in practical cottons, linens, or wools for their women's wear and the men generally wore grays or browns. The boy is dressed in a "skeleton" suit, which meant it followed the lines of the body, with no fluffs, puffs, or protuberances.

125. French bride and groom, ca. 1805.

126. George "Beau" Brummel, ca. 1805, and Percy Bysshe Shelley, ca. 1820, England. George Bryan "Beau" Brummel, left, an English wit and dandy who was a close friend of the prince regent, promoted himself into the absolute authority on men's attire of the period. He popularized dark, simply cut clothes, elaborate neckwear, and trousers rather than court breeches. The poet, Percy Bysshe Shelly, right, epitomized the look of the Romantic Movement, which stressed the casual in attire in pursuit of romantic adventure. Other key leaders in the Romantic Movement were the poets Lord Byron and John Keats.

127. French couple dressed for travel, ca. 1806.

128. French lady and gentleman, ca. 1808.

129. Young French couple in walking costume, ca. 1810.

130. Fashionable women, France, ca. 1810.

131. Three Empire evening gowns, France, ca. 1810.

132. Couple out for a stroll, France, ca. 1810.

133. Stylish French couple paying a call, ca. 1810.

134. A fashionable French couple, ca. 1810.

135. French couple in formal court dress, ca. 1813.

136. Fur trim and ostrich plumes, France, ca. 1813.

137. Two ladies wearing redingotes, France, ca. 1815.

138. Family in formal day wear, France, ca. 1815.

139. Day wear, Romantic period, ca. 1826.

140. Evening wear, Romantic period, ca. 1829. The lady's light colored evening gown with contrasting embroidery features a nipped waistline, a broad neckline to the shoulder, a full skirt, and short puffed sleeves—in two tiers in this case. Her hair is arranged in an "Apollo knot" and is elaborately decorated with metallic leaves. This plate shows the full tail of the gentleman's coat, which emphasizes the small-waisted look, further enhanced by a short waistcoat length in the front closure.

141. Women's undergarments, Romantic period, ca. 1830. During the Romantic period the tiny waisted look was achieved with serious corsetry with the additional aid of down filled pouches that were equipped with bands that tied around the waist and worn to the back. Also tied to a band around the waist were deep side pockets, which could be reached via slits in the side seams of the skirt. This illustration shows a lady in her under dress checking out her make-up before donning her outer garment. Her companion is already fully attired in a walking costume with a large ostrich-plumed bonnet. She is wearing *spatterdashers* (spats) to protect her hose from getting splashed with mud over her ballerina styled slippers.

142. Men's undergarments, Romantic period, ca. 1830. This drawing shows a gentleman being helped into his corset by his valet who is pulling tight the laces in the back of the garment. In a search for the perfect figure, gentlemen (as well as ladies) resorted to padding where needed for rounding the buttocks, the shoulders, the chest, or the calves (as shown here). He is applying tinted powder to his nose to reduce the shine and give a more languid look.

143. Sleeve variations, Romantic period, ca. 1831. In the Romantic period the bishop sleeve became popular for day and sports wear. The lady on the left is wearing a one-piece pelisse robe in a subtly colored polished cotton print fabric, which features a snugly fitted set-in waist and full skirt which falls to the floor, and balloon or bishop sleeves. The lady on the right is dressed for riding in a similarly cut gown of dark wool and a same color fitted waistcoat with bishop sleeves. The tiny buttons on her jacket were made of dried peas covered with the same fabric as the gown. Her top hat is of black silk with a green-tinted veil.

144. Boned corset, ca. 1837.

145. Evening wear, ca. 1837.

146. Day dress, ca. 1840.

147. "Pre-Raphaelite" gowns, ca. 1840–70. In 1848, the painters Dante Gabriel Rossetti, W. Holman Hunt, and John Everett Millais founded the brotherhood of Pre-Raphaelites in which they championed a return to the styles of the renaissance. The women in their circle wore gowns like the ones depicted in their paintings and the look became the "Ascetic Period" in fashion, which would persist into the 1880s. Both gowns seen here are based on Rossetti's paintings. The fabrics are vibrant colors taken from Renaissance tapestries.

148. Evening wear, ca. 1845.

149. Day wear, ca. 1848. Lady's dress of pale ice blue; white bonnet with pale blonde lace trim. Her parasol is a deeper shade of blue. Boy's outfit is black and white.

150. Evening wear, ca. 1849.

151. Amelia Jenks Bloomer's "rational" costumes, ca. 1849. On the left is a walking costume with loosely fitted top and bloomers; on the right, a day dress with a sashed waist and trousers. Her "liberated" ideas became the scandal of both England and the U.S.

152. "Rational" evening wear, ca. 1850. Two "Bloomer girls" demonstrate that evening wear was possible in the Rational Dress Movement. These shortened dresses with matching bloomers were made in pale colored silks with contrasting trim. The young men are wearing traditional evening tailcoats.

153. Evening wear, ca. 1851. Gentleman's black evening dress with a black silk waistcoat and white under-waistcoat. Black shoes, top hat, and cravat; white kid gloves

154. Lady's costume and child's dress, ca. 1852. Lady's claret red costume with black lace trim, white collar and cuffs, and pale yellow gloves. The bonnet matches the gown. Girl's dark brown jacket over a taffeta skirt of purple, green, and brown. White blouse, pantalets, and stockings; black boots.

155. Man's riding coat and lady's fur-trimmed day cloak, ca. 1852. Brown and black was a popular combination of the period, as were olive green and black, amber and brown, and deep red and black.

156. Woman's dress and man's "Prince Albert" frock coat, ca. 1853. Dress in pink, with black jacket and white blouse. Man's "Prince Albert double-breasted frock coat. Menswear was severely tailored in somber tones of brown, green, gray, or black in plain, striped, or checked woolens.

157. Crinoline dresses, ca. 1854. Lady's crinoline dress in rust-and-black stripes. White bonnet and blouse. Girl's navy blue jacket worn with a medium blue skirt, white blouse, pantalets, and stockings; black boots.

158. Crinoline walking dresses, ca. 1855. Woman's walking dress of taffeta; skirt edged with quilling of satin ribbon. Little girl's dress of barège (a sheer fabric of wool combined with silk, cotton, etc.) trimmed with silk braid, pantalets with crimped frills, muslin or lace.

159. Bridal wear, ca. 1855. The bride is dressed in white, by now a must. Her groom is in formal black evening wear.

160. Promenade costumes, ca. 1856.

161. Outdoor costumes, ca. 1857.

162. Day wear, ca. 1857. Woman's imported day dress with tasseled trim; young boys suit.

163. "At-home" wear, ca. 1858. Lady's at-home dress. Man's smoking suit worn with a velvet cap; the jacket was shown in a darker tone than the quilted lining and the trousers. The braid was probably gold.

164. Lady's riding habit, ca. 1858. Beaver hat

165. Woman and her children "at home," ca. 1859. Lady's tunic with braid decoration, white linen undersleeves, collar, and bowtie, worn with full skirt. Boy's collarless jacket, vest, and trousers. Child's kilt and velvet jacket with silk lapels, worn over white linen blouse and breeches.

166. Lady's promenade gown and U.S. midshipman's uniform, ca. 1859. Gown from *L'Iris* magazine. U.S. midshipman's service dress cap, jacket and trousers, navy blue; belt black; necktie black on white skirt. All buttons and insignia gold.

167. Carriage cloaks, ca. 1859. From *L'Iris* magazine.

168. Day wear, ca. 1860. Woman's day dress and man's costume from magazine *Les Modes Parisiennes*.

169. Lady's summer burnoose, ca. 1860.

170. Patterned evening gown, ca. 1860. Imported patterned evening gown decorated with roses.

171. Woman and child, ca. 1861. Woman's dress of apple green wool with brown fur trim and white blouse. Dark brown hat with red roses and white ribbons. Girl's dress, pantalets, and stockings in white with a pink sash.

172. Lady's opera cloak, ca. 1861.

173. "Turkey back" jacket and walking dress ca. 1861–62.

174. Woman and child, ca. 1862. Sprigged grenadine dress, skirt with four flounces, bound and headed with velvet; boys costume based on military Zouave uniform.

175. Promenade costumes, ca. 1862. Lady's promenade gown. Gentleman's single buttoned frock coat, held closed with only the top button, a style of the period.

176. Walking costume, ca. 1863. Walking costume in candy pink, trimmed with black ribbon and white eyelet embroidered flounces. Natural straw hat, trimmed with black feathers.

177. Ice-skating costume, ca. 1863. As featured in *Godey's Lady's Book.*

178. Woman's day dress and U.S. Army uniforms, ca. 1864. Officers' coats, New York regiment: navy with gold braid and buttons; trousers red; kepis red with gold braid.

179. Walking costume for the seaside, ca. 1865. Red cloak with white trim; white skirt with red appliqué. Natural straw hat with black feather, red hatband, and a pale blue veil. Yellow gloves.

180. Lady's Zouave-design robe and cape, ca. 1865.

181. Lady's "Alexandra" dress and U.S. Army captain's uniform, ca. 1865. Velvet trimmed mantle with guipure lace, and a wide guipure insertion with medallions. U.S. Army captain's blouse navy with gold ornaments; black belt with red sash; hat black; trousers medium blue; holster and cartridge case black.

182. Lady's military-styled dress and Confederate Navy commander's uniform, ca. 1865. Woolen robe dress with military print design. C.C. Navy commander's uniform: coat gray with gold braid, buttons and epaulets; collar gold with black edging; belt black with red sash; cap pale gray with black bill, band, and crown.

183. Winter promenade suit, ca. 1867. Heavy black silk, trimmed with narrow velvet tabs and jet buttons. Coat of black velvet with quilted satin lining. Muff and trimming are of grebe (feathers much like marabou). Hat trimmed with velvet ribbon and gold flowers.

184. Ball gown, with crinoline hoop, ca. 1868. The Crinoline Period ran roughly from 1850–1870. Like all fashions, in the hands of some, it became a travesty on itself, as seen here in this drawing of a lady being helped into her evening gown by two servants using sticks and stepstools to lift the gown over her "crin." In the foreground she is seen in her final glory in a gown by Worth. The first coal tar dyes had been synthesized in 1856, so the colors used would be bright and brilliant.

185. Evening dress, ca. 1873. Rose silk evening dress worn with a long apron overskirt of white striped grenadine, trimmed with lace. The bodice, bows, and roses are of the same rose silk. The border, puffed sleeves, and neckline are edged with puffed and gathered white sheer.

186. Bridal gown, ca. 1876. Cream-colored silk, trimmed with bouquets of oranges blossoms.

187. Undergarments for evening gown with bustle, ca. 1878. This illustration shows the underwear necessary for the bustled gown. On the right is the camisole-covered corset worn under full drawers. In the center is a back view of the bustle frame over a short layered half skirt, and finally is a long petticoat with layered flounces worn to cover the bustle frame.

188. Evening gown with bustle, ca. 1878. This illustration shows the lady in illustration 187 fully decked out in all her full bustled finery. The bodice is lace and the skirts are of silk with bands of satin ribbon holding ruched flounces. Corsages of silk flowers and ribbon hold up the overskirt and the underskirt is of finely pleated sheer.

189. Bustled walking suit, ca. 1877. Bustled walking suit with a gray silk underskirt, gray worsted overskirt and saque bound with silk and trimmed with embroidered bands and smoked pearl buttons. Gray chip hat with a red feather. Boy's suit of ecru cashmere wool; straw hat.

190. Bathing attire, ca. 1880. Bathing at the seaside enjoyed a new popularity in the 1880s. Men's knitted swimwear was considered quite daring because it revealed the line of the male anatomy so it was generally done in darker colors to soften the line. Women and girls swimwear fully covered the figure and in the 1880s women often wore their corsets underneath, even in the water. Navy blue with red and white trim were the most popular color choices.

191. "Aesthetic Look," ca. 1882. Oscar Wilde was the epitome of the now fashionable avant garde "Aesthetic Look," which was a direct descendant of the Pre-Raphaelites. He affected a velvet suit with a loosely fitting jacket, a soft collared shirt with a large, often flowing tie, and knee breeches. This suit had a quilted satin lining showing at lapels and cuffs. The female aesthetic generally wore dresses with no stays or petticoats and which were made of silks or Liberty prints in oriental type patterns and colors. The ladies generally affected a languid drooping appearance, which they considered "poetic."

192. Walking costumes, ca. 1884. Woman's walking suit of the third phase of the bustle, with a harder, more constructed shelf-like bustle layered over a straighter skirt, generally giving the impression of upholstery. The gentleman wears a boxy overcoat in the "Chesterfield" style over full cut checked trousers that taper at the shoe line. The girl wears a short version of the bustle.

193. American Victorian day wear, ca. 1885. The American versions of fashion were generally a little more flamboyant than their European counterpart, especially in the patterns of the fabrics. Notable is the apron worn under the bustle often its removal allowed the dress to serve as a dinner gown. Brightly colored plaids were a staple during the last half of the Victorian Era.

194. Seaside attire, ca. 1886. The lady wears a tailored princess line jacket with a minimal attached bustle over a pleated skirt. Both jacket and skirt are trimmed with contrasting colored silk ribbon. The man wears a boxy summer suit of lightweight wool blended with silk that has a high double breasted buttoned closure necessitating smaller lapels. His full trousers with the smaller ankle closures were called "peg tops." Both the man and woman wear straw hats called "skimmers."

195. Wedding attire, ca. 1890. By the 1890s the bustle had virtually disappeared. The small waisted bodice generally had some form of the leg-o'-mutton sleeve and the skirt was bell shaped, as seen in this bridal gown. Since it is a bridal gown it does have fullness to back to form a train. The young attendant has a shorter girl's version of the leg-o'-mutton with bell-shaped skirt combination that is decorated with ribbon loops and lace points. The little boy, probably the ring bearer, is dressed in a version of the then popular "Little Lord Fauntleroy" suit.

196. Evening wear, ca. 1891. In 1891 the "hourglass figure" was new and generally had a plunging neckline as seen in this sumptuous pearl-trimmed pale satin gown and fur collared manteau worn for the opera. The gentleman wears a long double-breasted evening coat with a set-in skirt. His collar is velvet.

197. Cycling costumes, ca. 1894. Bicycling was becoming a popular pastime for liberated young women. Here are two variations on the cycling suit with its leg-o'-mutton sleeves and billowing bloomers, which were most often seen in darker colors with white blouses and stockings (though sometimes white was seen).

198. Walking costumes, ca. 1895. Lady's costume with a bell-shaped skirt, pleated to the back for extra fullness, a tiny fitted waist, huge leg-o'-mutton sleeves and Art Nouveau trim. Her escort wears a high-buttoned single-breasted box-cut suit with peg-topped pants and a felt derby or bowler hat. Her gown would be in a medium to dark tone, while his suit would be in a dark tone.

199. Formal wear, ca. 1898. On the left, is a pastel-colored silk gown with a low décolletage, off the shoulder puffed sleeves, and a softly gathered train in back. Her stance is in anticipation of the "S" shaped silhouette popular in the first decade of the twentieth century. The gown on the right is by Worth and has an Art Nouveau scroll motif. It was stark black on white in the original. The gentleman has his opera caped overcoat on over his black evening suit and white vest.

200. Dancing attire, ca. 1899. The gown has a fitted bodice with a scooped décolletage and ballooned sheer short sleeves over elbow length gloves. Her full tucked skirt is edged with marabou and has ribbon and lace edged inserts of softly pleated sheer. Her hair is worn in what was then called the "Greek fashion," pulled back up and over the ears and then forward into a pompadour over the forehead. Her ostrich feathered hat is held in place with a sheer ribbon tied under the chin. The man wears a silk evening suit with spoon-shaped tail on the coat.